ACQUIRING LAND

THE DREAMSEEKER POETRY SERIES

Books in the DreamSeeker Poetry Series, intended to make available fine writing by Anabaptist-related poets, are published by Cascadia Publishing House under the DreamSeeker Books imprint and often copublished with Herald Press. Cascadia oversees content of these poetry collections in collaboration with DreamSeeker Poetry Series Editor Jeff Gundy (Jean Janzen volumes 1-4) as well as when called for in consultation with its Editorial Council and the authors themselves.

Also worth noting are two poetry collections that would likely have been included in the series had it been in existence then:

DreamSeeker Books also continues to release occasional high-caliber collections of poems outside of the DreamSeeker Poetry Series:

ACQUIRING LAND

Late Poems

JANE ROHRER

Edited by
Julia Spicher Kasdorf

DreamSeeker Poetry Series, Volume 17

DreamSeeker Books
TELFORD, PENNSYLVANIA

an imprint of
Cascadia Publishing House

Cascadia Publishing House orders, information, reprint permissions:
contact@CascadiaPublishingHouse.com
1-215-723-9125
126 Klingerman Road, Telford PA 18969
https://www.CascadiaPublishingHouse.com

Acquiring Land
Copyright © 2020 by Cascadia Publishing House LLC.
Telford, PA 18969
All rights reserved
DreamSeeker Books is an imprint of Cascadia Publishing House LLC
ISBN 13: 978-1-68027-016-7 ISBN 10: 1-68027-06-8
Book design by Cascadia Publishing House
Cover design by OfficeOfDevelopment.com

Library of Congress Cataloguing-in-Publication Data
Library of Congress Cataloging-in-Publication Data

Names: Rohrer, Jane, 1928- author. | Kasdorf, Julia, 1962-, editor.
Title: Acquiring land : late poems / Jane Rohrer ; edited by Julia Spicher
  Kasdorf.
Description: Telford, Pennsylvania : DreamSeeker Books, 2020. | Series: The
  dreamseeker poetry series ; volume 17 | Summary: "Continuing the saga
  initiated with her prior collection Life After Death, Jane Rohrer offers
  poetry recording her journey from a cloistered upbringing among
  conservative Mennonites and Church of the Brethren adherents to going
  "on the road, collecting places," as her title poem "Acquiring Land"
  describes it"-- Provided by publisher.
Identifiers: LCCN 2019043622 | ISBN 9781680270167 (trade paperback)
Subjects: GSAFD: Poetry.
Classification: LCC PS3618.O49 A64 2020 | DDC 811/.6--dc23
LC record available at https://lccn.loc.gov/2019043622

25 24 23 22 21   10 9 8 7 6 5 4 3

For Great-Granddaughter Mae

I did not think of death
the day that you were born,
so please be born again today
and every day hereafter.

CONTENTS

INTRODUCTION

"If somebody is not tenacious, I'm not interested. I want everyone to hold on with all four fingers, screaming!" During a visit in May 2018, I scribbled the sentence into my notebook as quintessential Jane Rohrer: fierce, precise, and frank as a fist—at least this is how I now see her, at the age of ninety.

And before? We met in the early 1990s, shortly after the publication of my first book of poems cast me with a set of much older people in a series of planned conversations that went on for several years concerning the relationship between our conservative Mennonite upbringings and creativity. Listening to the surviving tapes of what we called "the Creativity Group," I now realize that, although the sessions were organized by psychotherapist Lois Frey, and gregarious fashion designer Julie Musselman participated, the discussion was dominated by the voices of men: John L. Ruth, a minister and historian; Elmer Miller, a retired anthropology professor; Carl Keener (briefly), a botany professor and amateur theologian; and the painter Warren Rohrer, Jane's husband.

The Rohrers struck me as sophisticated and utterly secular, having long before drifted away from the Mennonite church in their pursuit of the arts and bigger ideas. Jane was irreverent, still frustrated by memories of a narrow-minded world she had been glad to leave. Warren, already living with leukemia for more than a decade, alternated between soft-spoken expressions of anger and grief. Perhaps the couple frightened me, living proof of the barter a Mennonite person must make in order to pursue the life of an artist.

In the all-or-nothing terms of their ethno-religious subculture in the 1940s, what other choice was possible for a Bible major at Eastern Mennonite College who wanted to paint instead of preach? What other choice was there for his bride but to drop out of college and become a mother and homemaker for a couple of decades? Nor did I see that in their own ways and for all of their lives, both painter and poet sustained the most intimate and daunting struggle of all: to make works of art that spoke with integrity, however obliquely, about their places of origin. That relationship is evident even in this new collection of Jane's work, where one poem recalls home scenes from a southern Mennonite family of the 1940s, and another transports an ancestor from the Appalachian hollows to "the Art Museum" (presumably in Philadelphia).

Whether at home or away, Jane is acutely aware of place, and she renders emotional and physical landscapes with intensity, concision, and diction that is unexpected and sometimes quirky. The emotional stakes are as high as her words are plainspoken, whether she writes of the death of her father or a sister's suicide—or of something as ordinary as the change of seasons. In "Home Movies," for instance, idyllic images from childhood prompt the speaker to demand, "Memory save me from my memories."

Grief and mortality preoccupy many of the poems, as befits an elderly widow, but they are also infused with wit and passion. This poet holds on and makes meaning of inevitable catastrophes, but she also reserves the right to switch verbal registers to the vernacular and make her escape. In "That Is All," a leaf left hanging onto a twig in autumn is figured as Christ on the cross, "stay if you want / crucified in place / nailed to the limb / with your unlined face," while the speaker insists, "I'm out of here."

The title poem also expresses the urge to leave but through a more meditative tone to arrive at something of a manifesto. It rejects the traditional, settlers' obsession with land ownership, revising the old ethic to mean not possession of place but the traveler's appetite for beauty and learning. Her lines glide on a smooth current of sound as the tourist acquires experience: "Last year I bought all the land along the Danube / Slipping into Budapest at dusk / As the lace curtains stirred gently / In the upper windows of the old Geller hotel." In a wonderful interview with her granddaughter included at the end of this book, Jane explains that, among other things, travel for her signifies flight from domestic duty: "enforced separation from the obligation to do what one is supposed to do at home." However tedious they may be, domestic tasks like pulling "Wissahickon grass from the lilies-of-the-valley" are their own kind of privilege, she admits in "Visiting the World." The high cost of touring, she realizes, is seeing the "inequity" that leaves the speaker unable to "look this world in the eye."

Jane's previous collection, *Life After Death,* was published by Sheep Meadow Press in 2002. A year later, six of her poems were included in *A Cappella: Poetry in Mennonite Voices*, an anthology edited by Ann Hostetler for the University of Iowa Press. In an article published that year in *Mennonite Quarterly Review*, Hostetler noted that Jane was one of the very first Mennonite poets—of any sex—to publish poems in a national literary venue in the United States, although she probably would reject the label "Mennonite artist." Jane was included in the "Creativity Group" as a spouse, and I regret that I probably regarded her mainly as Warren's wife or as a protégé of Stephen Berg, editor of *The American Poetry Review*. Maybe I turned from her story the way women often distance themselves from the terrifying struggles of their mothers until it's almost too late to name the obstacles they overcame or reckon with the sacrifices they made.

Now, as I approach the age Jane was when we met, I recognize the harsh constraints her generation faced—and value the heroic example of her lifelong negotiations among championing Warren's career, managing a family on their "toy farm," and finally tending to her own soul. The clarity of statement in the poems collected here is hard won and contains traces of the distance she has come and all she has brought with her to arrive at this brave voice.

"Let me know how I can help"; Jane offered the classic Mennonite woman's refrain at the end of her 2009 interview with granddaughter Willa. Her poems themselves are a great help, of course, boldly naming human experience. In "Widow," Jane describes her struggle to claim a voice that can roar (as a homophone for Rohrer), even as she anticipates the next mysterious journey:

> . . . I have come as my name
> from that safe jail
> have clawed through the membrane
> that was so tight   with only my skin
> against this spacious room
> in the cold
> I am as you   at risk of breathing
> skittery   windborne   free

I am so grateful for the opportunity to meet Jane again and to hear the tenor of her voice after all these years. It has been a pleasure to work with Christopher Reed and Joyce Robinson to honor her poetry—alongside Warren's painting—through the creation of two distinct exhibitions: *Field Language: The Painting and Poetry of Warren and Jane Rohrer* at the Palmer Museum of Art in University Park and *Hearing the Brush: The Painting and Poetry of Warren and Jane Rohrer* at Woodmere Art Museum in Philadelphia. These projects were made possible through support from the Palmer Museum of Art with funding from Penn State's Strategic Initiative Seed Grant in the Humanities, which also assisted with publication of this book.

I thank Michael A. King at Cascadia Publishing House and Jeff Gundy, editor of the Dreamseeker Poetry Series, for recognizing the importance of this project. As well, I appreciate the efforts of Jon and Prilla Rohrer, who endured many questions and visits with great cheer, and who also designed the cover; and Philip Ruth, who helped in countless ways as the work unfolded.

Mostly, I thank Jane for holding on, speaking up, and refusing to get "stuck in the mud." She's still traveling, even though it becomes increasingly difficult for her to leave the house.

—*Julia Spicher Kasdorf*

ACQUIRING LAND

I

HOME MOVIES

STORY

Don't think the story moves before us
like a single file of horses
passing along a horizon line in the eye.
Don't think there is a story at all
rather a great congress of scenes
on a stage revolving once in twenty-four hours.
It's theater in the round
and we are the audience
which is, of course, on stage also.
In a rare instant
when we are not performing
we see through the curtain
the act that just passed
in its slow merry-go-round motion
to the sound of calliope
and recognize ourselves
as we are, everywhere at once.

Films shot by my father in the forties
    flicker strangely on my TV.
I knew where I was this morning
but now I've gone from my life back home to the hills
    I see in snow and in summer
    the fields strung with miles of board fence
    lines in a drawing defining paddocks of horses
    studs geldings colts black bay chestnut roan
    nipping and playing now rising on hind legs
    in a slow impromptu ballet of elegant moves.
Look. Here the champion takes easily to the show ring
with my father up, as they say in the biz.
My father was always up, so to speak.

Memory save me from my memories.

I lean close.
We all walk in my mother's rock garden
of a Sunday morning before church.
Bells ring in steeples across the river
    but not in our plain church
    where the preacher sometimes grants my father a pew,
        sometimes not.
My sister puts the dog in the lily pond
    my baby brother in his white Sunday suit and little white hat
    rides a slick horse on the lawn.
Someone says it's Camelot. What a word.
Look. My aunts are all dressed up
    in large lovely hats
    at a family reunion in the State Park.
Someone steadies Grandpap, stepping on large boulders
    to cross a stream.

He wears a suit and tie and hat.

So many Sunday afternoons.
So many nights on the edge of dissolution.
Slowly other images from beneath the surface
        rise to take revenge
        until all that is left in the pile-up
        is the eternal limestone fields
        and the Virginia sky.

I strain to see the hazy icons come and go
        as through a redolent scrim.
We did not know how absolute and confused
        we were in our unconfusion,
        how rock-like, how immutable.
Any dream of mine for order in these remaining fragments
        remains useless.
        I thought I would survive the edit
        when the death of life ruined my history
        but I am a snippet on the cutting room floor.

It says on page thirty-five
of *Red Flannel Rag*
my great uncle Luther Kirkpatrick
was the meanest man in Hopkins Gap.

The poetry of the holler
is the subject here
and I must return there soon
to see if it still takes twenty minutes in June
from the instant sunlight leaves the valley floor
until darkness falls on the faded clapboard houses
and the clatter of moonshine stills.

Luther, what am I to do with you
now that you have been carried out of the mountains in a book
but seat you in my barrow
with all the other ancestors
I wheel daily along the streets of my life
to, say, the Art Museum
where you might feel at home
with the villagers of Hieronymus Bosch.

"The fog is thick and
I am having trouble directing traffic.
Constant rain is disconcerting, too.
And I am cold.

I know I said I'd tell you before I did it
but the telephone is out
and my computer has crashed.
I have taken care of things, though,
had my hair done, put on my diamond earrings
and brushed my teeth.
I would say I am ready for my close-up.
Near the mouth of the tunnel I feel warmth.
The pills look nice with my manicure.

Someone, sing to me."

Now we enter a terrible stanza,
an unfurnished room
where the dead do speak, don't say they don't.
It's a recital. The tape plays over and over,
(How are you? Everything is just fine.)
and she walks—
    like the Queen of England
    dangling her handbag,
    arms extended, probing the air,
    fingers in motion
    as though typing or playing the piano.

Everywhere I go I look for her.

The scene is lit by the thin light of a new spring
A scarf of green floats low in the ravaged Park
But even here by the hedge at the edge of my yard
I stand in danger.
I would like to shoot a short movie
And call it From Today To The End Of My Life
However, no camera could record the devastation I see.

The day of the storm the landscape streaked by
As if painted on the side of a high-speed train
And I was too close to the track.
It brushed my face.
Even now the chunks of order left at my feet
Settle daily closer to the drop-off point
Carved by floods rushing from the inlets of the City.

I am Rilke in Ronda at the Reina Victoria
Looking daily down the abyss by the hotel
That still shows the white wall with the green window
Framing his view of the gorge
Located somewhere between reality and legend
In his Spanish Trilogy.
Oh, I would exchange my chasm for his if I could
But I am planted here above the abyss I have been dealt
And who knows how many invisible abysses
Break in waves from my personal precipice?

I listen to sweet sounds of my life and look far down.
At the end, if there is an end
At the bottom, if there is a bottom
Stuff comes up out of the dirt.

The words *dappled with sunlight*
floated across the open field
as I drove by.
You understand the dapples
did not float
or the sunlight
just the words
since by that time
I had passed
and would never see
that green instant again.
Yet it is cut in permanence
and perfect
in my most real of archives
a small gallery
of moving frames
from another place
while I am here.

I rake leaves   it is fall
they are falling you see   that's all
      not dying or hearing a call
      just falling   that's all

The trip   the blue distance
      between the branch and the pile
      was too sweet a chance to glide
      and tack back and forth in magical style
      like men in hang gliders over La Jolla
      ecstatic and quiet up there
      but for the clicking of harness and wings
      in folds of air
      as they came down over us
      with that satisfied look
I've been away   out of my skin
                  out of my mind

So stay if you want
      crucified in place
      nailed to the limb
      with your unlined face
Me I'm out of here
(don't write   don't call)
I'm bored with it all but the fall   that's all

She lived years in grief's exquisite sphere
walking as the oxen walks   boustrophedon
in a small field   tended a garden
so miniature you could put it in a safe at night
and took short afternoon strolls
on the lawns of her memories
why, you could hold her and her whole world
in one hand   and shake it like a snow-filled paperweight
her mouth opens in a large O
her eyes register a slowed taking in of the world
as she runs out of air
in the low wintry light
of her permeable shell

but I have come as my name
from that safe jail
have clawed through the membrane
that was so tight   with only my skin
against this spacious room
in the cold
I am as you   at risk of breathing
skittery   windborne   free

There came a morning as I knew it would.
Let me not exaggerate here—
    the room is not sad
    nor is the computer
    or the family photographs all over the wall.
A pile of yesterday's mail lies on the table.
I could say there was bad news there
but, then, the envelope appears usual
even though perhaps it contains word of the end of hope.

There is no place to sling this snot
though I desperately want to get it off my hand.
I sit, sad, nostalgic, surfing my mind
to music of the Weather Channel.

Look, I'm not going to jump
from the famous McCallum Street bridge
or spend the day reading Rimbaud,
though I may play some Roy Orbison.
I will get into my summer pants
one leg at a time
and slide into my flipflops.
Then I will sit alone at the table
    with coffee in a white cup
    near a small vase of lilies-of-the-valley
    and read the *Inquirer.*
When the *Inquirer* seems quaintly local I'll move on
to the *New York Times*
and somewhere in the Arts Section
I will read about that poet
    who writes messages to the world
    and gets them back unread.

II

VISITING THE WORLD

Sixty years ago, my fiancé's parents
Were relieved he would marry a girl
Whose father owned a thousand acres.
They had their standards.
I see the Shenandoah now
Like a World War II movie, sepia toned,
And the river flows by the house someone owns.

The day came, on the toy farm in Lancaster County,
When I stepped out of my shoes
Stuck in the mud in a cornfield
Screaming the known world must be bigger than this,
And went on the road, collecting places.
Leaving after leaving, the only sure thing we do
But we do not know it.

My mind is filled today
With a whiff of Lisbon in the rain
And the marina where the white ship docked.
I had pitched past Gibraltar
All night in my berth
And thrown up my gorgonzola risotto,
But I would pitch and rock again tomorrow
Just to get to the white city
That whispers   Spain   I am not Spain.

Last year I bought all the land along the Danube
Slipping into Budapest at dusk
As the lace curtains stirred gently
In the upper windows of the old Geller hotel.
At the edge of earshot, I swear, voices of the dead

Float from Hero Square, flat, quiet and bullet-pocked,
Alive now in literature and the stricken whispers of the people.
Go all the way to the top of the city
In the yellow of October and listen
To the unrecovered, barely subdued,
Eternally sad rumble of the past threatening.

One day I was driven to acquire real estate
In the cool and cruel tomb of Rameses Six
There by the jackal performing his sacred rites
There by the hot sands of Luxor
That baked from my bones
Separation, darkness and the bent to putrefy in my own epoch.

I am permanently on the move like everyone else.
Wind blows my hair but I dare not stop.
I need more and more addresses.
On a cold day in Paradise I must have some place to go.

Now I see him lie dying,
Man who has been mean.
He's made his bed so low
                    so narrow-hard
                    so clean.
Now I hear him sigh, crying
In minimal light at five o'clock
                    so slow
                    so dryly old,
                         "I'm cold."

Oh, it is the same old thing.
Same old song you always sang.
Don't worry, you are safe,
I am not son, I will not murder you.

But
I am daughter. I can walk away.
"Walk," he said.
He said walk and I walked.
And I walked. And I am walking.
But
Comes some thought
Of virgin timber
And wild persimmons, father,
                    pod,
                    dried husk

Of random seed,
Small boat I see set down
At the edge of water
And, any minute now,
The journey weatherless,
My father.

This morning I walked on deck near a man
who announced his imminent peel-off into a doorway
with an almost imperceptible change
in the position of his feet
as though his brain had given advance notice
and they had put it on their schedule.
Near him a woman power-walked with toes turned in.
Lady, I can only guess.

There were signs in the months before he died.
He listed slightly
as though to some unspecific coordinate.
He listened, as to an alluring secret
not meant for me,
whispered in a cool, elegant accent.
I had the ear for it,
his gathering dream of an adequate dimension
out there, not here.

Perhaps he saw what I am seeing now—
water and sky together
the horizon uncluttered of our decaying bodies.
Only neatly disembodied people
could occupy real estate
of such perfection.
On the other hand, perhaps he came this morning
as the man I followed,
just visiting the human mess he had loved.

But I, hopelessly lost in life
and giddy with limitation,
missed every single clue.

Just look at the surface of that water.
A wave is allowed to distinguish itself
For only the count of a slow sigh
Before the sea takes it back.

God knows I tried to run away on this ship.
The steady rhythm of the waves
Would shush the incessant sloshing
Going on behind my eyes. You'd think.
But rumors continue from the continent
Ca-ching, ca-ching
E-mails of obituaries in alphabetical order.
Old harpies line up
Like vacationers going through customs
With grievance cards filled out.
They rail at me
Ask what I think I am doing, laughing like that.

Well, this is what I am doing here at the rail:
I shall rise like that wave
And laugh as long as I please.
Only when I anchor to that which claims me
Will I make my return
As the wave to its home in the water.

If you write a poem that blows out of the water
What I see now, send it to me
Otherwise I will just have to make do
With the hulking shoulders of a thundering sea
She-beast looming
Tongue lashing the beach to the dunes
A thick slobber of foam
Breaks off in chunks
And skitters down the sand,
An elegant transparent dust-ball sculpture by Lynda Benglis.

As soon as I fall asleep
I begin writing the script.
A fix of him
Will get me through the night
In my bed half warm.

My go-to story unfolds
As I glimpse him through a doorway, waiting.
We will dance to silly music
And embark on one of those ships
Booked full of lovers.

I should write movies, not dreams.

When we are called to board
I see his gait slow
On the way to the water's edge.
Even as I try to stay with him
I, only, am escorted to a peculiar falucca
Rising and falling on the sloshing river.
An impatient man gestures me forward
As in, "keep moving, lady."
It is as though I have chosen this against my will.
I see babies, bedded like nativity symbols
In a rude front compartment
Cooing and kicking here by Luxor
Within earshot of the daily wail of prayers.

Now I beg, "Entity many people call God,
Give me back my silly ship,
Don't push me down the Nile with the babies,
My head turned backward into the wind
Forcing my boat faster and farther from the shore
Where he stands exhausted as the dead come to be."

Reading *The River's Tale, A Year on the Mekong*
two words leap at me from page 68:
spice market.
By page 69 I know
I am not reconciled to the memory
of a street in Mombasa
where a shop keeper expended a morning's effort
on my purchase of two dollars' worth of cumin.
All my days in Philadelphia
as I pull Wissahickon grass from lilies-of-the-valley
or go to movies at the Ritz
this man rises, dresses, and reports for duty
just off the dirty street
where the tourist vans park
dreaming his two-dollar sale.

In an underground bazaar in Tunis
the bargaining sounds like bees buzzing
and a woman sitting along the main drag
lunges for a half-empty bottle of water
in a guide's hand.
I am sentenced to be only what I am, a tourist
I feel my skin shrivel
against the inequity
I will take home with me.
I cannot look this world in the eye.

I am the one on the back deck of the ship leaving the canal
The one crying at the opera aria and near to going overboard
In the music of the wake churning up.

Of what I saw and what I heard I can say little
Or reach back for what I mourn, to take it with me.
If I had stayed, and we never can,
I would have met them all
There would have been teacups and goblets as in the old days
And eventually I would have danced in a long swag of skirt
And Venice would have been as it is in the books
Written by English women.
Attachment would have fastened me to those stone steps
I bought and would lose.
How contradictory of me. I was hardly there
Certainly not long enough to leave.

Take my advice:
If you go for more than a minute
You will die for its decaying perfection when you leave
You will play the films over and over
And do things intensely
As though for the last time.
You will come to sound like a lonely cello.

But then I am not talking about Venice.

Will I arc on a velvet swing when I die
Will you be there when I go high
   above my ancient tree to the sky
Will I unbind the velvet ropes
   and loose myself from sweetest ties
   but not fall slowly into memory

May I go and go and go to that wide entry
   with no door in
   and no door out
   no north no south
All benevolent air above below about

   Sha la la

III

INTERVIEW

EVERYTHING
IS A STUDIO

A written conversation between Jane Rohrer and her granddaughter Willa Rohrer, April 2009

Willa: Do you think there is a relationship between the place where someone writes and the writing that they do? If so, how would you describe it? What power does a space have over us?

Jane: Yes. You know, sense of place and poetics of space, etcetera. Long years ago, when we lived on the farm, the change of seasons was a lot more in my face, and cycles defined the year. But, in a way, the community was confining, and that was the power it had over me.

Are you saying that you retreated, in a sense, to "space"—to the seasons (and presumably the landscape)—because the human landscape was oppressive?

Yes. On the farm, with the family, I felt no such constriction but the community [in rural Christiana, Pennsylvania] would rather have marched in Boy Scout parades, as I wrote early on, and they did regularly. We were just trying to live there more inexpensively, but there was a price. We were known as "those artists." As to the landscape, it was essential to Warren, and to me it was lovely, too, but I tended to find a psychological component that he did not.

Why don't you have a studio? Have you ever had one? Have you ever wanted one?

I guess a studio is very serious and all that. There is nothing more beautiful than a lot of books floor to ceiling, and scattered on desks and tables, photographs of poets you have known. But no, no one cares but the writer, except perhaps an interviewer, who could say, "I am here in the studio." Now, I do think a writer with an important output needs a space where he can leave great piles of papers without them being disturbed. It would affect the work if the writer had lots of children running around having fun and making noise, but since I have lived alone since your grandfather's death, everything is a studio.

What about when Grandpa was alive? Did you feel a need for a studio then? I will not include this if it feels too personal—I'm just curious.

I really didn't realize one could pick up a pencil to write a poem until I was in my forties. Certainly, Warren did not inhibit it. I guess I was just too timid. Also, [sons] Jon and Dean were out and about in the world more, and there was just more time for stuff like that.

About that time, I also started going into Philadelphia with Warren when he was teaching, and I took classes at Temple with Thomas Kinsella. Then I found out that Steve Berg taught [at the University of the Arts] where Warren did, so I barged in there and asked if I could audit. That was the first I knew of *The American Poetry Review*, and Stephen Berg founded it. I was flabbergasted. The rest is history. I realized I knew nothing about poetry and started reading all the time. Sylvia Plath scared me. And Anne Sexton. Steve talked about knowing Robert Lowell well, and I was so intimidated. Then there were the big three: Eliot, Pound, W. C. Williams. Not to forget Wallace Stevens.

I think Warren's drive to art was more urgent than mine because he fought his way into it earlier, and he had all those materials he needed a space for. Writing is simple and, for God's sake, does not require a "studio."

Do you think the studio is a bourgeois invention?

We're talking writers' studios here. Artists who use materials more complex than paper need space. I guess Vermeer was bourgeois in the physical way he lived, but that didn't protect him from tragedy and struggle. It's all about money, isn't it? I'm all for writers having lots of money as a result of their brilliance, and, no doubt, when they "arrive" they will have a large physical studio, perhaps several. So, a studio may be bourgeois, but it has nothing to do with good writing. Of course, it is difficult to know what that is.

What is your writing process like? Is avoidance or procrastination actually part of it?

Avoidance is a lot of it, because I just hate putting stuff on paper that is so bad I have to correct it out of existence, so I tend to write in my head as long as possible. It is like spinning out one little thread for a cobweb and trying to anchor it somewhere so that I can then design connecting paths to arrive at other parts of a structure. I am trying to put a structure where it is too empty in my head. I have called it building a paper house out of a life lived.

What do you think of the idea of your studio being a mental space? Is that too neatly convenient?

Of course, you have to have both a mental and a real place to work. When I travel I take my head and my canvas *New Yorker* bag, and that's enough for a working situation.

My addiction to travel is because it is an enforced separation from the obligation to do what one is supposed to do at home. Also, there is that strange phenomenon of feeling connected to any place in the world, no matter how exotic, because one does not stay there long enough to unload one's emotional baggage and spoil everything with longing and sadness. After all, one is there. If one stays any length of time, however, it becomes all too apparent that one is only a tourist and that is painful.

Traveling to Africa, and especially Egypt, for example, I found comforting because it has existed so long and gives us a record of human striving. I have never met a trip I didn't like, and when I am at home I miss every place I have traveled.

If travel is a kind of studio for you—or a way of being that inspires work—do you think that the ideal studio should actually give us an unfamiliar rather than familiar place in which to work? (I am thinking also of writers who have produced their best work while in exile—Joyce, Nabokov.) What do you think?

Travel is a smorgasbord of fresh visual stimuli, served up materially, as well as a lovely permission to goof off, especially when one is on a ship. It is looking at the water day after day and seeing no clutter. Great cities show us history aesthetically. I remember taking this boat to Delos from Mykonos, and walking around the footprints of entire houses, and the design was so perfect. They lived aesthetically. That old tourist trap, Pompeii, blew me away with its complexity. Yes, I find the *un*familiar more important, I guess because my insides back off when first in a new place. When at home, I find I have to get a little desperate to get up a head of steam to write.

So, Willa, hack away or throw away. Anything goes. Let me know how I can help.

Grandma

ABOUT THE AUTHOR

Martha Jane Turner was born in 1928 in Broadway, Virginia, the oldest daughter and second of six children. Her father, a prosperous poultry farmer and breeder of Tennessee walking horses, was distantly descended from the Scots and English Turners of Southern Appalachia. A conservative Mennonite, he was often in conflict with the church; her mother came from a more pious Church of the Brethren home. Growing up, Martha Jane (as she was then known) shouldered responsibility for much of the housework and care of her younger siblings.

Two years boarding at Eastern Mennonite (High) School in Harrisonburg, Virginia, offered a temporary escape, but Jane returned to help her mother with baby Charles for a year before enrolling in Eastern Mennonite College. She married fellow EMC classmate Warren Rohrer in 1948 and took a clerical job in the dean's office while he completed degrees in Bible studies at EMC and in art education at Madison College, both in Harrisonburg.

During the 1950s, the Rohrers had two sons in swift succession and moved to suburban Philadelphia. Warren taught art during the academic year and studied painting in the summers at Penn State. In 1961, they moved to a farm in Christiana, in eastern Lancaster County, Pennsylvania. By her own account, Jane devoted herself to growing and preserving food and homemaking until their sons became independent. Their farm, with its enormous garden and berry patch, was a favorite country destination for artists and collectors from the city.

During the 1970s, Jane turned to poetry: she joined a writing group in Lancaster, read voraciously, and audited classes at Temple University and the Philadelphia College of Art. Stephen Berg, founding editor of *The American Poetry Review* and her instructor at the College of Art, selected some of her poems for *APR*, and continued to publish her work throughout his tenure there. Jane submitted her poems to few other publications; her files include one rejection notice from *The New Yorker* and an acceptance from E. F. Dyck, poetry editor of *Grain*, the international literary journal published by the Saskatchewan Writer's Guild. Dyck, a former Mennonite, belonged to the 1980s prairie literary renaissance associated with Turnstone Press in Winnipeg, and his solicitation of her work—at least in retrospect—represents an early instance of the transnational literary conversation that became Mennonite/s Writing. But that would come later.

The Rohrers moved to Philadelphia in 1984, and Warren died in 1995 after a long illness. In 2002, when Jane was 74, her first poetry book, *Life After Death*, was published by Sheep Meadow Press, edited by Stanley Moss. He selected and ordered the collection, arranging the poems to stress Jane's devotion to her deceased husband and life on the Christiana farm. Together these poems surpass the specifics of Jane's biography, their elegiac tone extending beyond Warren's death to mourn contemporary culture's loss of connection with the land.

After Warren's death, Jane's younger brother Charles, a travel agent, took her on many international trips, and she has said that travel returned her to life and writing. Several travel-inspired poems appear in *Life After Death* as well as this current collection. All of the poems gathered here were previously published in *The American Poetry Review* after 2002 except "Acquiring

Land" and "Weatherless Journey," which first appeared in *The Journal of Mennonite Writing.*

Jane Rohrer continues to live on the edge of Fairmount Park in Philadelphia in the studio residence she renovated with Warren.